The Really Good Fun Cartoon Book of NLP

A SIMPLE AND GRAPHIC(AL) EXPLANATION
OF THE LIFE TOOLBOX THAT IS NLP

Philip Miller

Crown House Publishing Limited
www.crownhouse.co.uk − www.chpus.com

First published by

Crown House Publishing Ltd
Crown Buildings, Bancyfelin, Carmarthen, Wales, SA33 5ND, UK
www.crownhouse.co.uk
and
Crown House Publishing Company LLC
6 Trowbridge Drive, Suite 5, Bethel, CT 06801, USA
www.chpus.com

British Library of Cataloguing-in-Publication Data
A catalogue entry for this book is available
from the British Library.

13-digit ISBN 978-184590115-8

LCCN 2008921437

Printed and bound in the UK by
Printer's name and address
Gomer Press, Llandysul

Contents

i

The Really Good Fun Cartoon Book of NLP

A very brief introduction

I started studying NLP some six years ago. After the initial training, I wanted to learn more and read more about it. I bought a book and since then have added many more. On the whole, they're good, but I'm a simple soul and didn't like the use of jargon and lack of illustrations (I must be a visual person then, which just means I respond well to pictures).

This book is my attempt to get across, in a way that is simple, easy and fun, the really useful tools that are contained in the life toolbox that is NLP.

One last point, please don't treat the cartoons* too seriously. They're just meant to be fun and help get the points across. You might find some of them a bit zany! If you don't "get it", just smile anyway and move on!

PHIL MILLER, WARGRAVE, BERKSHIRE, 2008

* Information about the cartoons, and notes on the text can be found on pages 138–149.

Chapter 1

An introduction to NLP

What a weird name!

Let's just get the name thing out of the way – NLP stands for *neuro linguistic programming*. Because that's a bit of a mouthful, we tend to use just the initials. And – yes, I know it's weird, and yes, I know it's funny (peculiar, not ha ha) – but that's the name. So how come?

NEURO

Concerns the brain and the things that go on in your mind. Also the rest of the neurological system, including the five senses.

LINGUISTIC

This relates to language, both spoken and non-spoken (sometimes called body language).

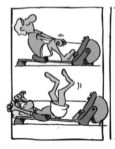

PROGRAMMING

This is about your behaviour and your thinking patterns.

From now on, we'll just stick to NLP!

What is it?

NLP is a collection of ideas and tools that can help you with your life. It can help you understand and cope with 21st century life more effectively.

On the front cover I've called it the "life toolbox". What's in that toolbox? I think that there are two main compartments in the toolbox: firstly, tools that are for understanding yourself; and secondly, tools that help you understand other people. The purpose for using these tools would be to have more effective communication, better motivation for yourself and others, and a more positive frame of mind.

The four pillars of NLP

1. Rapport – or being on the same wavelength

This is the cornerstone of NLP when you're involved with someone else. If you don't have rapport with someone, you can't communicate with them effectively. This is like the key that opens the lock in the front door of another person. (More on this in Chapter 7.)

It also means being in rapport with yourself – a challenging concept about being at one or being comfortable with yourself and with who you are, and who you want to become.

2. A sense of the senses

All the information that we use to make sense of and understand the world we live in comes to us through our five senses – what we see, hear, feel, smell and taste. How aware are we of these five streams of information coming into us all the time? (For more about this see Chapter 4.)

3. What do you want? (outcome thinking)

"Start with the end in mind." This is a really positive way of looking at things – thinking about what you do want and not focusing on what you don't want. (More on this in Chapter 15.)

4. Flexibility (in your behaviour)

It is okay to change your mind! One of the definitions of madness is to keep doing the same thing and expect a different result. If something's not working for you, do something different. This book is essentially about changing what you do so that you can get what you want!

Attitude, attitude, attitude!

Some time ago I ran my own business. When recruiting new people, we would focus on their attitude towards work more than qualifications or experience. It's just great to be around people who have a good attitude. Why is this? You're working with people who want to learn and improve their performance. As a manager, teacher or coach, it's so much easier and more rewarding if you're "pushing at open doors".

Five of the attitudes to have for studying NLP are:

Compare that to the world of TV soaps or tabloid papers where bad news and negative attitudes seem to be the norm!

HEALTH WARNING – the 3 Rs

Reg Conolly of Pegasus NLP Training uses this simple reminder - "the 3Rs". These are Respect, Reassurance and Recognition. Why do they deserve a place here? There are some powerful ideas in NLP and they can be used in ways which might be considered unethical. Understanding and influencing yourself and others is good, manipulating people is not. Thus the theme of the 3 Rs is:

- Respect other people.

- Reassure them if appropriate. For example, they may not be as posi-tive about change as you are.

- Recognition for the fact that everybody is unique.

Chapter 2

Ten interesting ideas

Introduction

NLP has a set of ideas that I think it's really good to have a look at and think about. They're not truths or facts, nor is there any proof that says they're right. They are just ideas, a way of approaching life. I'm suggesting that you consider them and think about how they might influence you and your life and possibly the lives of other people.

Your initial reaction to some of them might be "that doesn't seem right", but I'd like you just to put that thought aside and act as if they could be of interest to you. Be curious and try them on for size. Perhaps you'll discover another way of looking at the world and understanding your experience ...

There are quite a lot of these ideas, but I've picked just ten which I've found really helpful. I've split them into two groups: those that concern you as an individual and those that concern communication between people.

This for me is the essence of NLP – it's about understanding yourself and it's about the understanding between you and other people.

So what's the first idea?

Idea 1
There's no failure, only feedback

I think that this is brilliant.

We live in an age which can be very negative. Newspapers, TV and other media seem to focus on bad news stories; they want to undermine success, and they love failure and apportioning blame. This is exemplified in the culture of the TV soaps which dwell on things and relationships going wrong.

"There's no failure, only feedback" focuses on learning – learning from mistakes. If you don't have a go, how can you learn? If you model (copy) top sports people, they accept and learn from their mistakes (failures). In football a top striker knows that for every ten shots, maybe only five will be on target and allowing for the performance of the goalkeeper and defenders, that this will result in only one or two goals. So you might say that they fail 80 or 90% of the time, but they learn from every shot and they know that to get a goal, they've got to have ten shots, even if eight or nine fail!

There's a portrait of the playwright Samuel Beckett in the National Portrait Gallery in London with the quotation:

"Fail, fail again, fail better"

In business, the top entrepreneurs and managers know that they cannot get every decision right – indeed, 50% might be considered a good score in decision making. However, they will continually strive to learn from their "mistakes", to avoid them in the future, and just accept "failure" as part of the decision-making process.

How can we apply this to our everyday lives? In today's risk-averse society the fear of failure means not trying out new things, means sticking to what is known, in the belief that it will be safe and secure. However, that is hugely limiting, whereas having a go, learning from mistakes is a positive process that leads you somewhere new and brings about results in your life. There-fore, re-label "failure" (= bad) as "learning" (= good).

Idea 2
If something's not working, do something different!

Isn't one of the definitions of madness to keep doing something the same way and expect a different result? I know that this can happen to me, for example, when I get frustrated with modern technology (computers, mobile phones, DVDs ...) or when I am playing a sport, such as golf. For example, if I get stuck with a computer problem, I try to stop, have a glass of water, get a quick breath of fresh air, before going back to the problem. My knowledge of computing hasn't magically improved, but it's remarkable how the solution then happens! Or another example, a friend was playing golf and playing very badly. He said; "I've got to change and do something different." He then took off his sweater and started playing really well!

If you watch a child or teenager learning to use a new phone or a computer game, they approach it in a different way to someone like me (aged 60).

They just keep trying different things until they work it out – they're continually experimenting. If I get stuck in a loop of thinking "this should work", I'll keep repeating it until it does work – except of course, that it doesn't! Not only does that strategy not work, because it doesn't give us the result we want, we end up feeling bad about ourselves as well!

Learning to recognise the "hitting your head against the wall" feeling which comes from trying to solve a problem with an approach that doesn't work could be a great trigger. It tells you, "Now's the time to stand back – to stop and think – and to try an alternative approach." Link ideas no. 1 and no. 2 together – keep trying different things and you keep getting more feedback!

Idea 3
We have all the resources that we need

This, for me, is quite a tough idea! Again, it's recognising that point where you get stuck in a situation, thinking things like:

I don't know what to do.

I don't have the right tools or equipment.

I don't have the right materials.

You might get similar kinds of responses – or excuses! – whether doing a DIY project, painting a picture, trying to solve a business problem or making sense of your personal finances. (There is more on resources in Chapter 16.)

But what if ...

- You bought a book on balancing your finances (like Alvin Hall does on his TV programme)? Or talked to someone who manages it well?

- You took the time to read or re-read those DIY, self-assembly instructions , or you got someone who is good at DIY to read them and explain them to you?

- You looked at the internet for information and advice?

- You thought about networking? It might be true that you don't know anybody who knows about this, but you might know someone who knows someone who does know ...

- You were to use an imaginary resource: how would Shakespeare or Einstein or Gandhi have approached this? Just act as if they could give you some advice ...

Idea 4

If one person can do something, then anyone can ...

Another tough one! If I think of playing a golf shot as well as Tiger Woods or drawing as well as Michelangelo or singing as well as baritone Bryn Terfel, this concept stretches my belief in it to the limit! But if I rethink it to say that just occasionally I hit a great shot, or get a line just right, or really hit a note that I'm pleased with, then this idea is starting to help me.

On TV these days, there are many programmes in which people are coached into doing things that they never dreamed they could do, such as dancing, singing, ice skating or rock climbing – and by the end of the programme, voilà, they're doing them!

Research shows that the vast majority of people "know" that they cannot draw. Drawing courses are available for those who cannot yet draw. They follow six simple exercises (based on Betty Edwards's book *New Drawing on the Right Side of the Brain Workbook*) and 90 minutes later people demonstrate to themselves that they can indeed draw. Their reaction when they realise this is just fantastic!

Idea 5
We all make the best choice available at the time ...

At Cranfield University School of Management. Andrew Mawson (now Lord Mawson) has been a guest speaker on a number of occasions and talks about his experiences of bringing about social change in his community in the East End of London. Of dealing with civil servants he says, "These are not bad people, it's just that they don't necessarily take the best decisions ..."This happens to all of us – it applies to me, and it also applies to other people: we think we're acting for the best, but it just doesn't turn out that way ...

So when you're frustrated by what someone has done, stop, take a breath (and a sip of water if you want) and remember that they thought at the time that they were making the best choice available. After all, no one deliberately makes mistakes. You just hope that they are following Idea 1 and learn from what happens!

Idea 6
Mind and body are one system ...

Are you a people watcher?

Do you find other people fascinating?

We'll be looking at body language in later chapters, but just think about these three pairs of characters and the emotions that they are displaying – what do you think they're feeling?

How you feel and how your face and body look are interlinked. Sometimes how you arrange your body will prevent you from having certain feelings. For example, stand with your neck bent forward so that you're looking at the ground, and try to smile ... When you're being happy and joyful things are literally "looking up"!

If you feel tired and depressed, doing some physical exercise is a great way to get out of it. I go to a keep fit class on Monday evenings. In the middle of winter when it's cold and wet and there's a nice fire and something good on TV, it's very easy to persuade myself that, "I'm not feeling 100% and shouldn't really exercise ..." However, I usually persuade myself to go ("It'll catch up with me" or "I'll only feel bad about myself") and I always feel great when I get back – not just physically, but mentally as well – plus, to be honest, I normally stop for a pint in the pub on the way home ...

Idea 7
People operate in their own unique map of the world

One of the great ideas of all time – people operate in their own unique map of the world. Or put it another way: we're each unique, all 6.5 billion of us! Yes, we're obviously physically different, but what this idea is saying is that mentally we all operate with a different map of the world that we hold in our minds.

Yet how often do we remember that? When I used to get upset that people couldn't follow my train of thought, my old boss Brian used to say, "Everyone's logical, it's just that their logic is different to yours."

You and I may be in the same place, for example, in the garden, but we process the information that our senses are receiving differently: you see the flowers and hear the birds; I begin to sag at the thought of the grass that needs cutting. Have you ever been in a meeting with a colleague and when you discuss it later, you wonder, "Was he in the same meeting?" because his view of what happened was so different from yours?

Is it any wonder that we sometimes don't understand one another! Help is at hand! Just realising this is a great start. We'll be exploring the stages of the process in later chapters.

Idea 8

The map is not the territory ...

This idea follows on from the previous one. When you're communicating with someone, you're dealing with their view of the world, not the "actual" world. In fact, what you think of as the actual world is just your perception of it, your map, isn't it?

I visit a local nursing home to see my father. When I go in through the front door and rub in the hygienic hand gel, it's a signal that I'm entering a different world, a parallel universe if you like. To the residents, time has very little meaning: which day of the week it is or even which week of the year. Sometimes they play bingo. They can't hear the numbers as they're called out, or they can't see their cards very clearly. Some have great difficulty covering the numbers that they have on their cards. Frequently they jog their card and then they have to go through all the numbers called again. To an outsider it may seem like mayhem, but the residents obviously enjoy it! It's bizarre, but if you're going to join in, you have to switch off your world or your map and navigate using theirs!

Now this may seem like an extreme example, but when you think about it, isn't this the way we all operate?

Who knows what goes on in my mind, or yours, or anyone's? And yet don't we all think we do sometimes? And if we believe we're right ... well, we'll come to that in Chapter 9.

Idea 9

You cannot NOT communicate ...

Whatever you do or don't do, if someone is within sensory range (normally they can see or hear you) you will be communicating to them, even if you don't intend to! Even doing "nothing" communicates something!

It's also very difficult, unless you're a good actor, to think one thing and say or indicate something else ...

Idea 10

The meaning of the communication is the response it gets ...

"I communicated perfectly, they just didn't understand me."

"Are you deaf?"

"If I've said it once, I've said it a hundred times ..."

Ever heard or said something like this?

This idea, "The meaning of the communication is the response it gets", places the responsibility for communication on the "sender" of the message and not on the "receiver".

HEALTH WARNING! If I don't understand someone, then simply quoting this as a slogan will not help the situation. In fact, it can make it a lot worse! Therefore think about applying it to *yourself*, not for criticising others!

Chapter 3

What are you like?

Introduction

We've discussed the fact that we're all unique. Our physical differences are there for all to see, but what of the mental differences?

How else are we different?

What is it about our personalities that make us different?

We're going to look at a useful tool, *the personality map (the name used by Reg Connolly at Pegasus NLP Training)*, to help us understand our own and other people's personalities. A good way to think of this is to imagine an onion with many layers. In some ways, we're like an onion – the more you get to know someone, the deeper you move down through the layers of their being. For example, when you meet someone for the first time, you'll probably talk about the weather or the journey that you've just had. It's unlikely that you'd talk about politics, religion or spirituality.

Why is this idea useful?

It really does help when communicating with someone to have some idea of what is important to them for each layer. For example, someone might say, "I have to work outdoors", "I don't believe in smoking because it's so bad for your health," "I just want to have a good time," or "My family is everything to me". These factors of someone's personality clearly have an impact on how you might approach them and communicate with them, be it socially or at work.

The personality onion (or map)

There are six layers to this particular onion. The first two outer layers are the ones you can observe by how the person appears, and by what they say and do. The other four layers are below the surface and you get to know them over time, more by inference.

Another analogy would be that the first two are like the part of the iceberg that you can actually see, the other four are the part of the iceberg that you can't see, the part hidden below the surface.

The first three layers could be said to relate to the head or mind and are public areas, whereas layers four to six, the inner three, relate to the heart, the inner self or personal area.

Environment is about external factors concerning factual details about your context: where you are, who you are with, which aspects of time are important. For me, for example, I think best sitting in the garden. Some people work best in the evening, others in the morning. Some people like to work outdoors by themselves, some people like to go into town with their friends to enjoy themselves.

Behaviour is about what you actually do and say. There is a difference between "I surf", the action of surfing, as opposed to "I am a surfer", which might imply something about a carefree lifestyle and particular style of dress. Other examples might include: I play tennis, I drink wine, I cook, I care for my mother …

Capabilities are quite specific: it's about skills, knowledge and talents. It might refer to things that you do well and like, or about things that you're not so proud of. For example: I am able to shoot a score of under 80 at golf, I can draw well, I can play the piano to Grade 5 standard, I can programme the video or DVD, I can drive a car and have passed my driving test.

Beliefs and values are the fundamentals that guide your life. This is like the inner core of a reactor, it's about what's important to you, what drives you at a deep level. It could include things such as:

■ valuing the importance of family and friends

■ choosing a lifestyle that promotes good health and physical well-being

- having fun
- committing to the beliefs of a religion
- believing that learning and education are important
- believing that money is everything
- believing that money isn't everything

Identity is getting a sense of who you are deep down. Many people will go through life without ever really asking the question "Who am I?" and yet this kind of understanding can help you if you get stuck with a decision about a new direction. For example, if you have to choose between two jobs or decide whether to live in the town or country, ask yourself: "Am I the sort of person who ...?"

Purpose or "What's it all about?", "What's my purpose in life?" is a huge question that most people will probably never ask of themselves. What's your vision or mission for your life? This is the deepest layer, and one that you may never share with another person.

Clues for understanding someone else's layers

Listen and watch!

Remember you can see and hear the consequences of someone's behaviour that takes place within a particular environment. You can find out about their capabilities during normal conversation: "How did you learn to dance like that?" Beliefs and values are trickier and it may take some time before you know someone well enough to ask, "Why do you dance?" or "Why is dancing so important to you?" And understanding someone else's identity ... well, that's a lifetime's occupation.

How to use this information

This story invites you to think about modern life and about how the personality map might be useful. There was a solicitor in Edinburgh who had called in a consultant to look at his business. It was a small business and the consultant knew that in a small business it is important to get to know the owner and what he or she wants to achieve. The discussion started with the facts and history of the business: his father had been a solicitor and had wanted his son to be a solicitor. The son had done as his father wanted, had become a solicitor and had duly taken over the practice. The consultant then asked the key question: "Do you enjoy being a solicitor?" A seemingly innocuous question, but one which made the solicitor really stop and think.

He replied, "Actually, now that I think about it, no. I became a solicitor because that's what my father wanted." Further discussion continued about what he really wanted to do and it eventually came out that he really wanted to be a photographer. Having realised that, he quit the law, went back to college to study photography and in due course become a photographer.

What's the point of the story with respect to the personality map? Many of us, like this solicitor, just get on and do what we do. If we do think about it, we might just think about the three outer layers. It may not be that until we enter "the zone of uncomfortable debate", such as when the consultant asked the key question, that we start to think about our inner layers and really question why we're doing what we do.

So you could use this to help someone else work out who they are and what it is they really want to do with their lives. I'd caution that this is not to be done lightly. And remember those 3Rs: respect, recognition and reassurance. Initially, it's probably best to think about applying it to yourself – moving slowly and carefully down through the layers. If you want to change, understanding your personality map is a great starting point.

Motivation and de-motivation

If you're a parent, you're probably aware that when you tell off a child, you're supposed to say, "that was a naughty thing to do!" rather than "you're a bad boy". How does this relate to the personality map? Well, the first statement is about the child's behaviour, whereas the second is about their identity, which is a far more serious level. You are not your behaviour! The man in the earlier story was a solicitor for many years, until he recognised that he was really a creative person.

Motivation

If you want to influence another person, you can do it using your knowledge of the six layers of their personality map. Each layer will have its own "hot buttons" – triggers that will get them to move towards what they want more of in life. So if you can find someone's "hot button" – being pampered in a spa, opportunities for trying new activities such as bungee-jumping, receiving presents such as chocolates, roses or diamonds, or a desire to be praised, or opportunities for personal expression through the arts – then you've a big clue as to how to motivate them. Relate this back to the personality map.

De-motivation

Conversely, doing something that upsets, annoys or just doesn't work for someone is a great way to de-motivate them! Normally, best avoided. For example, my daughter worked for a company that was quite strict about good timekeeping, sticking to the company guidelines as to when holidays could be taken, not abusing sickness absence. She accepted these rules and thought that they were fair. Imagine her reaction, when over a period of many months, her supervisor repeatedly left work early, had excessive time off for sickness (particularly on Mondays and Fridays) and took holiday during the busiest periods. Not only did this behaviour not motivate her, but it de-motivated her, so much so that she eventually resigned.

Chapter 4

A sense of the senses

Introduction

We've already discussed in Chapter 1 that all the information we receive comes to us through our five senses. Interestingly, we tend to favour one of the senses as a way of creating the map of reality in our minds. This usually means one of the three main senses; seeing (or visualising), hearing (or auditory) and feeling (or kinaesthetic). A good cook might favour one or both of the other two senses, smell and taste.

"How does that look to you?"

"How does that sound to you?"

"How do you feel about that?"

The kind of language people use can give us valuable clues about how we think and about how others think. This is a big help in building rapport and communicating. Let's examine (or "look at", "talk about" or "see how we feel about") this in more detail.

Visual

As you might expect from the fact that I've illustrated this book with lots of cartoons, I have a preference for visual thinking. And because you've chosen to read this book it may even be that you're strongly visual too. On the other hand, my wife Penny, whose preferred thinking style is kinaesthetic, doesn't really grasp the cartoons. I'm able to visualise things – a cartoon, a redesign of the garden, a golf shot or a tennis serve. If you wanted to sell me something or persuade me about a concept, then physically using a drawing or mentally helping me to paint a picture would be a good idea. You could use words such as:

Imagine, see, visualise, picture or paint a picture, put you in the picture, different point of view, lightbulb moment ...

And if you or I wanted to enhance these concepts, we'd add more description:

Crystal clear, bright or dim colours (or black and white), sharp, hazy, 2D or 3D, one or panoramic images, moving or still images

Do you get the picture?

Auditory

A client recently sent me an e-mail about a proposed meeting. It read, "Sounds good to me". A good clue about his preferred thinking style. Now, just one phrase that anyone might use is not enough in itself, but it gets me to focus on listening hard to the exact language that he uses to look for other clues (and yes, that's my preference popping up again – I *look* for them).

Hear, clear, noisy, harsh, talk, orchestrate, music to my ears, that strikes a chord with me, you're clear as a bell, sounds good to me, listen and learn, poetry in motion, I hear what you're saying ...

And again, more detailed description might include:

Loud or quiet, harsh or soft, low or high notes, fast or slow, melodic or discord, accented or neutral, calm or emotional (voice), continuous or intermittent, near or far

How does that all sound to you?

Kinaesthetic

In my experience of running training courses in business, most of the people who turn up have a preferred style that is either visual or kinaesthetic. This is not a scientific or statistical fact, it's just based on what I've experienced (and it probably says something about unconscious rapport and liking, which we'll discuss in Chapter 7). People whose preferred style is kinaesthetic tend to take time to experience or feel an idea. They may take more time to think about something. So the speed with which they process information or ideas is a clue, as are the words they use:

Feel, soft or hard, comfortable, firm, warm or cold, fluffy, it hit home, get a feel for, get hold of, get a grip, pain in the neck, solid as a rock, feels good to me, keep in touch, deep impression …

Plus, we could enhance those feelings by also using: *whereabouts (in the body) – head, heart, guts, intensity – strong or weak, temperature – hot or cold, duration – sustained or brief.*

How do you feel about that now?

Non-specific

Some senses are non-specific, i.e. they're things we sense inside ourselves. For example, described by words such as: communicate, understand, seek, think, experience, contemplate and imagine.

Multi-sensory experiences

In reality, many experiences combine some or many of the above. You have to be curious and just wonder which particular sense interests you (or someone else) the most.

When the pre-Christmas *Radio Times* arrived last December, it had this multi-sensory description of a Christmas feast prepared by the famous chef, Heston Blumenthal:

- *Mulled wine – hot on one side of the glass and cold on the other*

- *Gold, frankincense and myrrh – langoustine, onion and vermouth stock cubes, wrapped in edible gold leaf and dissolved in frankincense water, served with a spoon carved from myrrh*

- *Babe in a manger – communion water sprayed with the aroma of freshly washed baby*

- *Flaming whisky sorbet – served amid the perfume of a wood panelled room with a roaring fire and a leather armchair*

- *Hand reared roast goose – fed on apple powder, Paxo stuffing and essential oil of Christmas tree*

- *Hand reared roast goose – pommes purées with goose, chestnut and bacon, served in a bell jar containing the aroma of roasted chestnuts*

- *Reindeer milk ice cream – frozen in liquid nitrogen (of course ...)*

I'm salivating just writing about it!

Chapter 5

Anchors in life

Introduction

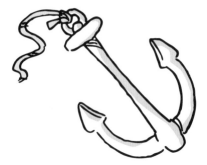

Have you ever had the experience of hearing a piece of music or smelling a distinctive smell that immediately takes you back to a particular time or event? This type of experience is called an "anchor". The surprising thing is how quickly your mind takes you back there – it might go back many years, but seems like it was just yesterday. Wow! However, this can be good news or bad. The good news is that you use an anchor to take you back to a pleasant or positive experience, and the bad news is that it could also be an unpleasant or negative experience.

Let's have a look at some examples:

I'm a non-smoker. The mere sight of someone smoking, particularly as they get anywhere near me, triggers a negative reaction. Even now, just writing these words, my face is screwing up and my mouth is turning down – and there's probably not a cigarette within 50 yards of me! That's the power of an anchor!

On the other hand, if I want to be calm, tranquil and at peace with myself and the world, I just visualise myself sitting in the garden on a summer's day. That nasty facial expression has just vanished!

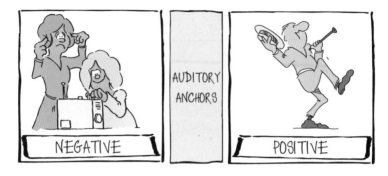

Last summer I sang in a choir, in public, for the first time. What a great experience. (I'd believed that I couldn't sing for over 50 years of my life – more of that in Chapter 13.) I was singing 'Oklahoma' at the top of my voice with 30 other people. I'm smiling again just thinking about it.

Loud, raucous (sounds that I don't like ...) pop music takes me back to conflicts with our children about their music.

The feeling of sand on your toes might take you back to happy childhood holidays by the sea. This might also be a multi-sensory anchor, which makes it even more powerful: the cry of seagulls, the heat of the sun, children playing on the beach, the noise of the waves breaking, the taste of salt spray on your lips and the sea-weedy seaside smells, plus all the sights of the sea and the beach. I have a photo of a sandy beach on my study wall and just by looking at it I can get a real sense of what the sand feels like – and guess what? I'm smiling again!

Whereas certain things (worms, snakes, spiders ...) might take me back to very unhappy or scary events. I've just thought of fingernails running down a blackboard (a feeling and auditory anchor) and I'm back in my (bad) 13-year-old school class. My teeth also now feel awful – excuse me a moment while I go and clean my teeth ...!

Back to smoking. Even the smell of cigarette smoke (and especially of a stale ashtray) is bad news for me, and I'm out of there as fast as I can! On the other hand, a positive anchor such as a specific smell (aroma) of cooking that I associate with a particular period in your life – for example, mother's home baking – and I'm drawn towards the kitchen!

Taste is also a very powerful trigger for anchors. Just think of something that you really love the taste of ... and how difficult it is to stop eating it. But that's enough about chocolate; think of something you don't like the taste of. Does this take you back to a particular time or event? School dinners anyone? Again, by way of example, I don't eat eggs because of a bad childhood experience.

Drinking beer on the other hand, makes me think of being with friends having a good time ...

How to use this

An anchor is the stimulus that triggers the memory – be it good (positive) or bad (negative). I coach someone about his business. His is a tough business sector to be in, sometimes this can get very depressing after a long detailed discussion. To change his mood, I just ask him if he went sailing at the weekend (he's a keen sailor). His whole state changes instantly. He smiles, he relaxes and enjoys talking about his latest experience – it's like he's back there reliving it and just forgets his work problems.

If you want to get out of one state and into another (for example, upset to relaxed), just "call up" a positive anchor. I don't know what will work for you, so just experiment – have a whole range of anchors that you can choose from: pictures on the wall, your favourite music, objects that you can handle, a whiff of perfume …

Another NLP technique for changing something you no longer want to do could be summed up using a visual analogy with your computer. Let me explain. You're in a negative state. Visualise this as an image on your computer screen. Now click on the minimise button to make it disappear from the screen. Have a number of positive anchors already minimised and click on one of those to maximise it to fill the screen (this is a magical computer screen that allows you to have multi-sensory images, i.e. sounds, touch, taste and smells as well as sights …). Voilà! You've replaced your negative anchor with a positive one. You may have to repeat this several times to get it to work.

Final thought

I've just spent an hour relaxing in front of the TV after a hard day's writing and watched an episode of the celebrity chef, Rick Stein's *Mediterranean Escapes*. The last scene showed him back in Cornwall recreating a Moroccan dish (a tagine). As he prepared it, he smiled and commented on the fact that at the sight and smell of it cooking he was instantly transported back to Morocco ...

Chapter 6

Different points of view

Introduction

Have you ever had one of these thoughts?

- "Why don't they understand me?"
- "Why don't they listen?"
- "Are they deaf?"
- "That's not what I meant at all!"

Do you remember anything like that? Have you wondered what they were thinking? What was going through their mind? If you can get this other perspective, this other point of view, it can be a really powerful tool from the toolbox in your communications with other people.

- Wouldn't it be good to have a two-way conversation where both people feel their point of view is being heard?
- Wouldn't it be refreshing to avoid "assumptions" about what you'd thought you'd heard or they'd meant?
- How much better would it be if relationships could be improved and built upon, even with "difficult" people?

How to do this is the starting point of many communication and influencing processes.

The process of thinking about both points of view

Remember a conversation that you had recently that didn't go as well as you would have liked – it could have been work related or something in your personal life.

If the conversation took place seated, sit down and face an empty chair. Visualise the other person sitting in that chair. Now recall the conversation step by step. What was the context? What did you say? How did you say it? How did you feel at the time? What were the other person's responses? How did you react to what they said? How was it left at the end of the conversation?

Now leave your chair, walk around a bit and go and sit in their chair, the one where you imagined them to be, so that you face the chair you were just in. Assume the posture that they had during the original conversation. Literally put yourself in their position in every way that you can: how they were sitting, how they looked and how you think they were feeling (I know that you don't know, but just have a go!). Now relive the conversation again from their point of view. How did they speak? What did they hear? What did they see? How did it make them feel? How did they respond to this?

When you think that you've had a good go at this, stand up and walk around again. And then move back so that you can see the two empty chairs. Pretend that you are a "fly on the wall" (an invisible or neutral observer) during that conversation. What would you have seen, what would you have heard? What was going on between these two people? How do you think that both parties felt afterwards?

I use this exercise a lot on communications training courses. People find it really powerful, particularly when they're in the observer position.

The outcome that I hope you've got from this is that you realise that some-times (only sometimes?) we tend to see things very much from our point of view. Taking a bit of time to think about the other person's point of view can make a real difference to how you approach a situation and can lead to a much better dialogue and mutually acceptable outcome.

The Stuffometer

A new word! A new idea!

The Stuffometer – it's a device to represent how much of your thinking is either about **your** stuff or **their** stuff .

MY STUFF + THEIR STUFF = 100%

The dial goes from 0% MY STUFF which means your attention is totally on the other person (i.e. 100% THEIR STUFF, something which only happens for very brief moments) to 100% MY STUFF, which means you are totally absorbed in yourself (i.e. 0% THEIR STUFF, something which probably hap-pens more often).

Consider the Stuffometer in any communication!

Think about:

- ▦ Was I just putting across my point of view?
- ▦ Did I check understanding?

- Did they understand?

- Did I listen to their point of view?

- Did I consider their point of view?

- How did I respond?

An example might be a salesman. A poor salesman might only be thinking about his presentation and not listening to his prospect – so his MY STUFF reading will be high, say 90% and THEIR STUFF will be low, say 10% (remember, the two figures should add up to 100%). He's only thinking about himself and not the other person's point of view. Conversely, for a good salesman, his MY STUFF might only be at say 25% when he's making his presentation (THEIR STUFF would therefore be at 75%) because he's concentrating on their needs and responses.

I know it's just an idea, but just think about that Stuffometer inside your head. How far round the dial was the pointer? Was that what you intended?

Chapter 7

Getting on the same wavelength (rapport)

What is rapport?

What comes to your mind when you ask yourself the question "What's rapport all about?" When I run a training course session on rapport, I ask people the same question. Here's a summary from a recent course:

- On the same wavelength

- Tuned in

- Real vs phoney

- Empathy

- Trust

- Two-way understanding or two-way traffic

- Engagement

- Building relationships

- Common ground

- Their context
  - Situation
  - Issues (knowledge gathering)
  - Respect them

- Comfortable

- Humour (where appropriate)

- Authentic

- Culture

- Body, voice and language matching
  - Voice (pace, volume, pitch)
  - Mirroring

- two ears/one mouth

How does that list compare to yours? Do you agree with all those points, or just some of them? Do you have some additional ones?

Let's have a look at rapport!

You know what it's like when you meet someone, possibly for the first time, and they dive straight in and start talking about the matter which most concerns them, but without any small talk or any effort to get to know you. It's unsettling, isn't it? It doesn't feel right. Maybe you're thinking, "I'm not quite ready for this." Maybe you're wondering, "Who is this person? I don't know who they are yet" – rather than listening to what they're saying. In business, I've sometimes noticed this with people who have technical skills rather than people skills, and especially with bad door-to-door sales-people.

Well, rapport is about avoiding this! It's so important to get on the same wavelength before you get into the meat of the conversation. Indeed once you achieve this, you also need to keep it going!

"LIKE LIKES LIKE" It's important to find common areas of interest with the person to whom you're talking and minimise the differences. I'm a golfer, so if I meet someone new and think they might be interested in talking about golf, I always ask, "Do you play golf at all?" If they don't, talking about golf is normally an instant turn-off, so I'll need to find another potential area of common ground. Conversely, if they do play, I can develop the subject to get the conversation going.

The thing about rapport is that it's a skill that can be developed. We can all learn about how it works and improve our ability.

Why is rapport important?

Do you get the feeling sometimes when you start to talk to someone (or even just before) that you'll get on? We'll be looking at body language in Chapter 11, but it might just be something as simple as a smile or the way they're dressed ...

I think that women are better at this than men – in particular, the way they give a small smile when meeting another woman for the first time.

We tend to gravitate or be attracted towards people we consider similar to us (watch people at an event like a business conference or a theatre crowd at the bar), because most people basically seem to prefer people who are most like themselves in some way or ways.

This could be why I seem to attract only certain kinds of people to my training. They want to be with someone who sees the world in a similar way.

What a great skill to have: to feel relaxed quickly and easily in someone's company! It does feel good to be in rapport with other people as you become "one of us". It's probably natural with close family and friends, so the trick is to develop that feeling with others. And one way to do that is to look for similarities with other people, rather than their differences (more on this in Chapter 12).

"No rapport = no communication"

No rapport means no communication. This is the view of Reg Connolly at Pegasus NLP Training. It may sound a bit extreme, but from careful observation, I think it's right (but check it out for yourself).

Some examples of this that work (or rather don't work) for me are:

◻ Talking to someone chewing gum.

◻ Talking to someone who is smoking (I'm a passionate non-smoker).

◻ Being neglected by someone when they answer their mobile phone. What makes it worse is when they use an excuse such as, "It's my mobile" (well what can you do?), "This is important" (and I'm not?). Even if we were in rapport, for me it instantly breaks rapport.

◻ Or how about someone who points or wags a finger at you? What does that do for you?

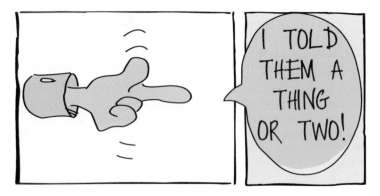

◻ Do you hear?

◻ Do you listen?

◻ Do you understand?

◻ Do you agree?

◻ Did you think, yes that's right?

◻ Did you think, yes, I do need to change my behaviour?

◻ Do you act?

... or none of the above! HEALTH WARNING – avoid these kinds of rapport-breaking activities yourself!

The "how to" manual

 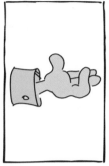 

Rapport is a skill that can be learned, so let's look at how we can do that (apart from not pointing a finger at someone ...).

The first two steps are very simple:

1.   Watch the other person.

2.   Listen to them.

Then you can start to match (or copy) them. HEALTH WARNING – this must be done subtly!

3.   Then concentrate on their eyes.

Match their eye contact pattern (by this I mean the portion of their time that they have eye contact with you).

Two extreme examples of this I know are the computer programmer who looks at the ground the whole time, and at the other end of the spectrum, a friend who is a seemingly intense entrepreneur who stares intently at your eyes the whole time. (As an aside, I found this very off-putting to start with, but I soon got used to it.) Most people come somewhere in the middle.

4.   Then look at other aspects of them.

    a.   Posture (body, arms, legs, inclination of the head, shoulders and hands).

    b.   Facial expression.

    c.   Direction of their look.

    d.   How their eyes move.

    e.   Breathing (speed, depth, high or low).

    f.   Body movement and gestures.

5. Match your voice closer to theirs. Again, be subtle. Don't try and imitate their accent, for example! I tend to have a very loud voice, so if I'm speaking with someone who's speaking quietly, I try to speak more quietly than I would normally.

Then perhaps, think about the more detailed aspects of their voice:

- Pace
- Pitch
- Tone
- Intonation

Again, be subtle. Do enough to feel that you are in rapport with them. I think that this is really important in phone calls. As an aside, I've noticed that people really hear a lot when they're listening to you at the other end of the phone – yes, they are aware when you're using your computer at the same time, and yes, they can hear you having a sip from your coffee mug! Therefore, it might be best to avoid these habits if you want to have good rapport with them!

6.   Language is also important.

a.   The patterns (visual/auditory/feelings) – see Chapter 4 for more on this).

b.   The exact words that they're using.

7.   And probably the most important:

Develop a genuine interest in the other person and what they're saying! If you find this challenging, start by wondering what kind of map of the world they have created for themselves. What's important to them about what they want to communicate?

In order to "get inside" the other person, it does require you to concentrate, listen and watch them (see also Chapter 8)!

Lastly, sometimes you want to break rapport. Why would you want to do that? For example, you need to get rid of that bore at a party or close the meeting because you're running late ... If you don't want to appear rude, break eye contact, glance at you watch, or at a business meeting, start getting your papers together (subtly) ... And if subtlety doesn't do it for you, simply say "I've got to go" and leave.

Develop skills and practice

To develop your learning about rapport, you can become a student of your own and other people's rapport skills by becoming a people watcher (if you aren't one already). No excuses for not having any examples. Those two people you see at a party, the couple at the restaurant, or the people round a conference table – are they in rapport?

To get you thinking while you're reading this, have a go at this simple quiz:

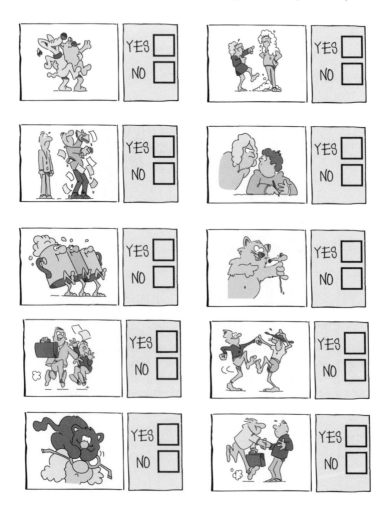

ARE THESE CHARACTERS IN RAPPORT?

Lastly, think about how you can give yourself some specific things to do to improve your rapport skills. For example, after a work meeting or spending time with someone socially, just review what happened, not from the point of view of the subject matter or content of what was discussed, but from the perspective of rapport ...

- When we were in rapport, how good was it?

  - poor, okay, good

- How much of the time were we in rapport?

  - none, some, most or all of the time

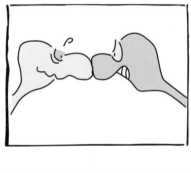 

Chapter 8

Listening skills

Introduction

Listening skills isn't really an NLP topic. I don't know of any other NLP book that has this type of chapter in it, but for me, this is one of the crucial building blocks of understanding NLP. If you don't listen to someone "properly", you can't really understand them. If you get nothing else out of this book, listening and watching are the two key foundations to good communication, in my opinion!

When we listen effectively we get better quality information and a better understanding of it as well. Good listeners also positively encourage others and consequently upset fewer people. This means less frustration and a more satisfying life ... for all concerned!

We all listen all the time, and yet we don't. With the radio/TV/mobile phone/iPod world in which we live, there always seem to be choices. Why do we need to listen say, at work? I suggest lots of reasons, including: building teams, developing people, during change, in conversations, in coaching and in sales.

The four levels of listening

The concept about listening that I want to offer to you and then develop is called the "four levels of listening" (Julie Starr, *The Coaching Manual*). It also uses the Stuffometer idea that we first saw in Chapter 6.

The first level is cosmetic listening

- Children listening while watching TV or texting

- "Mmm ..."

- "Yes dear ..."

- The listener's Stuffometer is at about 90%

In other words, cosmetic listening is just for appearances sake – it's not really listening at all.

The second level is conversational listening

- For example, in the pub, listening, then watching other people, then listening, then watching other people ...

- "Yeah, okay ..."

- The listener's Stuffometer is at about 60%

- Listen/think (stop listening)/listen/look ...

The third level is active listening

■ Listen, the words trigger a thought, you write a note (for example, a good work conversation)

■ Very focused

■ Recording relevant facts

■ The listener's Stuffometer is at about 30%

■ Paying attention

The fourth level is deep listening

■ Totally focused on "them" and not "you"

■ Getting a real sense of who they are

■ No writing!

- No input other than really good listening
- The listener's Stuffometer is at about 10%
- Giving full attention

Listening skills exercises

I've not included many exercises in this book as it's not primarily that type of book. However, I've made an exception with these two listening skills exercises, as I've found them to be the most powerful for participants at the training courses that I run. So using these two exercises let's get curious about how well we listen.

- The first exercise gets us thinking about when we've been using each of the levels.

- The second exercise gives us an opportunity to experience deep (level four) listening from both points of view (speaker and listener).

Exercise 1: The four levels of listening

Work on your own for five minutes.

1. Pick a typical work day from earlier this week or last week.

2. Go through the day:

   a. At home with your partner or with the family before work

   b. At work, with colleagues, with customers

   c. Whatever you did after work in the evening

3. How many conversations did you have?

4. List them.

5. Rate each conversation with one of the four levels of listening that you think each fell into (your subjective assessment – just have a go!).

   a. Cosmetic

   b. Conversational

   c. Active

   d. Deep

Activity	Level
At breakfast	
Journey to work	
First arriving at work	
At home in the evening	
An evening social event	
Totals	

1 Cosmetic	2 Conversational	3 Active	4 Deep

6.   Total up your day. Make a note of your highest area.

7.   Summarise the results … (you may find that level 4 listening isn't listed at all).

Deep (level 4) listening is rarely used by many people and yet it can be a very powerful experience; it helps us to calibrate the four levels. I'd encourage you to have a go at this next exercise. You'll need to work with someone else. To do it properly will take about two hours!

Exercise 2: Deep listening

Deep listening is not something that most of us use every day. However, it is an extremely powerful and simple technique that allows you to really understand the other person's issue(s), to have a real insight into them and get a sense of who they are. They will feel the benefit of being listened to properly and it's sometimes amazing how "just listening" can solve problems!

Julie Starr's exercise will give you a taste of what deep listening can be like ...

You will need someone else to help you with this exercise, find a willing partner and follow these instructions.

1. A (speaker) is going to talk about something (problem or situation that they want to change) for 10 minutes. They then repeat this for a second issue (another 10 minutes) and then a third issue (another 10 minutes). They're talking for 30 minutes in total!

2. B (listener) may ask questions, clarify information and acknowledge the points raised (e.g. by nodding).

3. At the end of those 30 minutes, B takes a further 10 minutes to summarise back to A:

    a. What the issues were, i.e. what they heard.

    b. How they, the listener, felt about it.

    c. Anything else about the conversation.

4. Then A gives B feedback about their listening for about 5 minutes (BE SPECIFIC):

    a. How well did the listener give you their full (100%) attention?

    b. How well understood were you?

    c. Did the listener have any effect on you?

    d.   How do you feel about the issues now?

5. Rules for the listener:

    a.   *Your role is to listen and understand.*

    b.   *Do NOT give ideas, solutions or suggestions.*

    c.   *Do NOT refer to your own experiences.*

    d.   *Do NOT attempt to direct the conversation.*

    e.   *Do NOT try to impress them or look good.*

    f.   *Remember: your role is to listen and understand!*

Swap over

Now it's review time! Consider how you felt when you were listened to properly. Where was your Stuffometer?

Think of a time in the past when you were not listened to properly. What impact could this have on your friends, colleagues and family?

Think of a time in the past when you were listened to properly (or from the deep listening exercise above). How good did it feel? What could you do to help you when you want to be a really good listener? Consider linking this question to an image of your Stuffometer down at 10% (this is an application of the anchor concept from Chapter 5).

Chapter 9

Now pay attention ...

Introduction

We've thought about and hopefully practised some listening skills, but what exactly are we listening for? People use language in lots of different ways, so by listening carefully to what they're saying and how they say it, we can get some clues as to what they're thinking. The assumption that I'm making here is that this additional information over and above the content of what someone is saying is useful in helping us to communicate more effectively because we have a better understanding of them.

It also enables us to ask questions to explore and check exactly what they mean. This is particularly useful, for example, if you're coaching someone. By reflecting back to them what they've said, it enables them to clarify their thinking. I know that this might sound a bit bizarre, but it can work. Have a go, try it out on someone you know (tip – start with a topic that's not too controversial!). When applied to yourself it enables you to think and speak with more clarity and precision, and to be less ambiguous.

Let's start by looking at some of the patterns that people use:

DISTORTIONS | DELETIONS | GENERALISATIONS

We'll split these patterns into three main categories – distortions (where the meaning of an experience is changed), deletions (where information is missed out) and generalisations (where logic is used in an illogical way). Sometimes it can be difficult to distinguish between these three!

Distortions

How can a letter upset me? It is only a piece of paper!

But if I allow the contents of the letter to upset me, I have chosen to become a victim; I am denying my responsibility for how I choose to feel. I can blame it on the letter or on what someone said or did, whatever. They love this distortion in TV soaps: "He does my head in." These distortions are a great excuse for us, aren't they?

Here someone is attaching meaning. What happened was that someone didn't say anything – the attached meaning is that it was a deliberate act to annoy me. You end up with a formula of *this means that*. If this meaning is something which applies only in their map of the world and not in yours – that is, there is no shared reality – then you need to check out their thinking. The question to explore this further asks how they reached that conclusion.

Here a judgement is being made without any supporting evidence. The responsibility (or maybe blame) is put onto an anonymous third person. Classic judgement statements might start with a phrase like "They say ..." which is a way of passing the buck. For example, "They say you're not good enough to be promoted" or "I'd love to give you a pay rise, but the management won't let me." Challenge such vague statements by delving deeper into what's happening, by asking for evidence, to find out about who these other people are and whether what they say is valid.

Mind reading is something we all do all the time (Doh! that's a mind read!). In Chapter 6 I asked you to do this deliberately, because some mind reading can be extremely useful, just as long as you realise you are doing it. You're second guessing what someone else is thinking. You're making assumptions about their thought processes. Sometimes they'll be right, but not always. It's when you act on what you have assumed about the other person that problems can arise.

You might be in a relationship where you're thinking, "He should know how I feel about this." In effect, this is projecting mind reading. Reflecting the mind read back as a question can be a good way to challenge the assumption that they do indeed know what you're thinking.

Deletions

Often information is just left out. We tend to do this a lot, because otherwise it may take forever if you're going to mention the molecular and biological nature of the milk you're going to buy from the corner shop! To speed things up, and get to the shop before it closes, we delete a great deal of what we could potentially talk about. In fact, most of our language is a kind of verbal shorthand; we assume that the other person will understand it. If we can't make sense of it, then we need to ask for more information.

Here the person speaking has not specified the details of how they know. Asking for the missing information needs to be done carefully (HEALTH WARNING – be very careful if trying this at home!).

Better compared to what exactly? The comparisons are not specified or are merely implied. In any questions, if appropriate, you need to ask what the alternatives were and why they weren't as good.

Here information about the subject has been missed out. Who has said what and when isn't given. Asking for the missing information can sound critical if it isn't done with care.

Generalisations

Generalisations are our fixed ways of thinking and behaving. Life is full of generalisations, because we need to have an understanding of how the world works. This is how we build our maps of reality. It would be very difficult if we had to work it out from scratch each time. But as with everything else that we "know" about the world, sometimes we're wrong, or we have created a "rule" based on only one example!

Generalisations tend not to invite change! Prejudice would be an extreme example of basing belief on small amounts of evidence. For example, "All purple people are lazy" (based on two purple people that I worked with ...). Or, more subtly expressed (and blaming someone else for the opinion), "Don't get me wrong, I like purple people, in fact some of my best friends are purple people, but they can be lazy."

The counter-statement above ("We didn't when you were on holiday") is a good rejoinder. Extreme examples and/or the use of humour can also work well. This might help them realise how absurd a universal rule could be. I also like to make the response absurd – in the example above, what if you said something like, "Would anyone die if we tried it another way?"

Rules are great, aren't they? "I must ...", "You should ..." or used indirectly, "The government should do something about this!" These rules might come from strongly and long-held beliefs, so challenging them too directly might lead to conflict – so perhaps something like "What would happen if all dogs didn't always have to chase cats?" might be better than the stark "Says who?"

Assumptions and presuppositions are used all the time in general conversation and especially by people such as politicians being interviewed by the media. It's great to learn to recognise these when used by others and you can use them to improve your ability to persuade people. If we think the person making the statement is "important" then we tend to assume that the presuppositions are true. To challenge presuppositions, ask for more information.

This statement has generalised things because it implies that there can never be any gain without pain – it's as if it's set for all time in a block of stone! Trying to get behind the belief might help here.

Why is there no gain without pain?

Did something happen that led to this belief?

Could you help them think about or remember a situation where a reward brought about an achievement or gain instead – thus invalidating the generalisation?

We'll look at limiting beliefs further in Chapter 14. These particular gener-alisations deal with what we claim is impossible. As such they limit what we can do and the options we have open to us. But really, this reflects more on the limited nature of our personal map of reality; it's just that we have arbitrary boundaries based on limited life experience. So how do we get the other person to go beyond their existing boundaries and explore their "no-go" areas? Get them to consider the benefits if they were to do that: What would we be able to do that we can't do now? What's the worst that could happen if we did try and it went "wrong"? (Remember that we learn from our "failures".)

Maybe all we need is a hand to hold. So who do we know that we could get to help us, to come with us on the journey into the unknown? Here's a story: A few people in our village wanted to get together as a fun choir. We knew we needed a good musical director who would be able to work with inexperienced singers, but no one could think of anyone who could do it. We despaired of ever getting the choir off the ground, but we remained open to possibilities. And then some months later, "out of the blue", Wendy (the choir's secretary) met Ros (a professional singer) at a party in the village and Ros agreed to become our musical director. The choir has now been going from strength to strength for over a year under Ros's inspired (and very patient) leadership!

Conclusions

Learning to listen "between the lines", so to speak, being curious about what's being said and thinking about why it's said and the way it's said (and not just the content) can give us many clues as to how someone thinks. This gives some real benefits in communicating with others:

1.   More precision in the communication.

2.   Facilitates checking understanding with the other person.

3.   May help the other person to get their thinking straight.

4.   Helps you check your own thinking.

This sets the scene for thinking about and planning the language that you might choose to use. Which leads us into the next chapter.

Chapter 10

It's not just what you say; it's how you say it ...

Introduction

We've covered a lot about listening in the past two chapters, but what of the language you use yourself? How can you phrase or articulate something to make it better understood or to make it more persuasive (if you wanted to persuade)? We're going to look at eight different examples of how you can use language to be more persuasive (HEALTH WARNING – you must use your judgement and remember the 3Rs to prevent persuasion becoming manipulation!).

Example 1 – Linking ideas

Smoothly linking two ideas can be a powerful tool in persuasion. The smoothness comes from the language that you use and the way that you say it. All these eight examples probably work best when you pay attention to the tonality of your voice – soft and quite quiet is a good place to start.

Example 2 – The subtle command

Here a command or instruction is made (slightly) more palatable and acceptable, by using the form of a question. You could even try it more obliquely: "It's drafty in here." There are many subtle ways of using language which seem like polite ways of phrasing commands!

Example 3 – The subtle use of a question

The subtle use of questions can really help in communication. This, for me, is one of the great practical uses of an NLP tool. I use it particularly when I'm coaching. Try it yourself or try it on yourself first – notice the difference between saying "Tell me ..." (which tends to be used with slightly harsh or demanding tonality) and "I'm curious to know ...?" or "I'd like to know ...?" or "I'd like to understand ...?" (which tend to be used with much softer, gently enquiring tonality). It's so much more subtle, less intrusive. Depending on tonality, a phrase like "tell me" or even "please tell me" can really put someone's back up and have totally the opposite effect to the one you want.

Example 4 – How we respond to negatives

One of the great lessons I learnt from studying NLP is that the human brain does not hear negatives. At first this just doesn't sound correct. But think about saying to a child "Don't touch that!" – what happens? There's a good chance that they will touch it!

Think about sport – say you were playing doubles tennis and you're about to serve and your partner says, "Whatever you do, don't serve a double fault!" What do you immediately start thinking about – "Serve a double fault ..." It's as if it draws your attention to the negative aspect of what they've said and therefore has the opposite effect to the desired one!

However, as in the cartoon, you can also use this when you what to influence someone to do something (and also recognise when someone is using it with you). Again tonality and voice inflection can really help to get your point over "You don't have to do it now ...!" (with emphasis on the "have" by saying it slower and by differentiating it in some way, for example, slightly louder or softer ...).

Example 5 – The power of the quote

HEALTH WARNING! – here comes another golf story (except that it's not really about golf)! Anyway, I was about to play one Saturday and while we were waiting to start, John, one of my playing partners, said that he had seen Colin Montgomery (one of Europe's best golfers) giving some advice earlier that week on Sky Sports TV. John said that Colin had said that the number one problem for club golfers (the amateurs like me, not the good professionals) was holding the golf club too tightly, which causes tension, which means that you don't swing smoothly. Because John was quoting a well-respected authority, I took this advice very seriously. I also put it into practice, had my best round for many months and won the Saturday afternoon competition! If John had said to me, "Phil, don't grip your clubs so tightly", I may or may not have taken the advice. Indeed, I might have taken umbrage at someone else telling me what to do.

You may have noticed the effect of someone saying to you (or someone else), "Let me give you some advice ...", particularly with the addition of a wagging finger. And how often have you offered advice to someone else without first establishing rapport to find out if they want to receive it from you? Simply pontificating, regardless of how exactly you say it (tonality, body and face language, context), is not necessarily a great way to win friends and influence people.

Example 6 – The use of presuppositions

You want someone to do something specific, but without giving them free rein, so you presuppose a limited number of options, which you list (to save them the effort of thinking!). In the cartoon, the presupposition is that "I am going to eat you ..."; the forced choice is between now and later – other options, such as not being eaten at all, are ruled out.

Those of you who have ever done any sales training may also recognise this as "the alternative close". The salesman never actually asks you if you want what they're selling (you might say no). Instead they ask, "Would you like a blue one or a red one?", "Will you take it with you, or shall we deliver it for you?", "Do you want one case or two?" and so on.

We frequently use presuppositions like these, but most of the time they go unnoticed. I don't know whether you'll notice these language patterns immediately or whether you need to think about them. The idea here is to make you more aware of them so that you can develop your own skill in using them (but only if you want to ...) and to be more aware of when other people use them when talking to you.

Example 7 – Metaphors

I love stories and metaphors; I think of metaphors as very, very short stories. It gives you the opportunity of rephrasing something for someone to make it easier for them to understand. So, for example, you might be trying to explain something to a work colleague and you see a puzzled frown appear. You might try using a metaphor or analogy to help them: "Let me put it another way, you know what it's like when ..."

I used several metaphors when describing the ten ideas in Chapter 2: the four pillars, cornerstone, key, lock, front-door, map, onion ... And in Chapter 5 I used the computer metaphor.

I think that this works because it puts the responsibility on you as the speaker to get your message across in the most entertaining way.

Example 8 – Last but not least, stories

My experience is that people love stories, especially if the stories are good stories (and not just about golf !). If you see a glazed look appear on someone's face, you might be overdoing it – this has been known to happen when I try to tell golfing stories to non-golfers as well. People are captivated by stories, so if you can use a story to get across the point you're trying to communicate, that can be very powerful and is more likely to be remembered. Therefore I suggest that you develop a repertoire of useful stories and metaphors that will help you do this.

At Cranfield Business School where I spend some time teaching, business stories are called "case studies" – but they're still stories. I think that they work because you're using someone else's experiences as an example. This means that the listener then has the choice (and responsibility) whether they choose to see if the point you're making (via the case study or story) might apply to them. Again, like so many of the previous examples, the difference is that you're presenting your ideas non-confrontationally. You're suggesting or implying ideas, you're giving the listener the choice, not just telling them what to do or think. Well, actually, you are – but you're doing it nicely, with rapport, in a way they'll enjoy.

These are all really powerful influencing techniques. They may appear quite innocuous, but as with so much of NLP, practise them to see how well you can improve your use of these simple tools.

Chapter 11

Language without words

Introduction

I'm indebted to Lauren (the famous character from Catherine Tate's TV comedy programme) for the catch phrase, "Look at my face, am I bovvered?" It's become a classic and encapsulates the study of body language in a nutshell. We all know exactly what she means, don't we?

I'd like to extend the phrase body language and introduce two nuances – face language and eye language, because I think that's where we get most information from when we're in conversation with someone. I've noticed that the sports commentators and pundits have started using and commenting on the body language of footballers or cricketers as they view from afar, but when we're talking to someone it's the face and particularly the eyes that we're scanning a lot of the time.

More picture quizzes!

WHICH EMOTION IS WHICH?
QUIZ 1 – BODY, FACE AND EYE CLUES

1. FEAR
2. ANGER
3. SADNESS
4. LOVE
5. CURIOSITY
6. BOREDOM
7. WORRY
8. GREED
9. CONFIDENCE
10. DETERMINATION

WHICH EMOTION IS WHICH?
QUIZ 2 - FACE AND EYE CLUES

1. NAUGHTY
2. EMBARRASSED
3. HAPPY
4. APPREHENSIVE
5. HOPEFUL
6. CURIOUS
7. PUZZLED
8. FRUSTRATED
9. SHOCK
10. FEAR

To get a sense that these quiz pictures are just about the face and eyes, try covering up the body part of the picture with your fingers.

The eyes also tell us a lot don't they? What they tell us we instinctively know, but if we study eyes we can enhance and improve these skills.

If this is of interest to you, try an experiment with a couple of friends. Get one to talk to the other about something they're really interested in. You sit off to one side, so that you can watch the eyes of the speaker without getting involved in the conversation. Just note how their eyes move. You may notice that they flick very quickly, mainly up and down, but also sometimes from side to side and you realise just how much eye movement is going on. Of course, the eyes keep moving in order to stay lubricated, but there seems to be more to it than this.

"So what?" you might think. Well, can you notice any link between the eye movements and what they might be saying and thinking? For example, when people are visualising something, their eyes tend to flick up or they tend to look up. I remember being told off at school when the teacher said, "The answer's not on the ceiling, Miller!" – I'm very visual and that is where I visualise a lot of things, so that was exactly where I saw the answer!

When people go into themselves to see how they feel about something or their "self talk" tells them something, you may notice that they tend to look down. In my experience, the eyes flicking to one side or the other is more unusual, and this might be that the person is hearing something.

105

HEALTH WARNING – when you're looking at someone's eyes, please exercise restraint! Having your eyes stared at isn't usual and can send out the wrong signals!

Chapter 12

A filtered view of the world

Introduction

We discussed early on that we're all unique and that we all operate according to our own individual map of the world. Here's another set of ideas that can help us understand ourselves and others: the kinds of things we pay attention to, the preferences we have for dealing with the world – in other words, how we filter information. NLP has described lots of these filters; one common example would be that which distinguishes the optimist from the pessimist.

Does someone see the glass as half full or half empty?

Are they consistent in this view?

Are there circumstances when they might see it the other way?

In communicating with someone, understanding their filters is a great way to help you know where they're coming from. It helps you to see and understand their point of view so that you can adapt your style to more closely match theirs. It is, therefore, another aid to help you establish rapport.

I also think that there's a parallel with psychometric testing here. You might be familiar with names like Belbin, Myers-Briggs Type Indicator (MBTI), and Thomas International (DISC). A good book (also very visual) that examines over 60 personality traits is *The Personality Profiler* by Claire Gordon. It is also good fun.

However, we're going to look at just five of these filters:

Filter 1 – Towards and away from

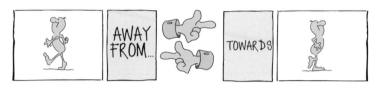

Have you noticed that some people are very focused and driven? They have very clear goals or objectives. They have a vision for themselves, maybe their business or their family's future. They can be dynamic and exciting people to be around, things get done and happen. However, they may not stop and think about potential problems. They may tend to steamroller objections. These are *towards* people – they know what they want and they tend to say, "I want ..."

Away from people, on the other hand, tend to focus on what they don't want. They tend to complain a lot. They can be very good at foreseeing problems and solving them. They're probably not very good at goals, as all they can see are all the things that can go wrong. Overall they seem a bit negative!

In conversation, simple questions will help you to discover whether someone tends to be towards or away from. For example, "What's important to you in buying a house?" – *towards* might focus on the kind of house they would like to live in, be optimistic about the rise in house prices, whereas *away from* will tell you what's wrong with where they live now, and might worry about the difficulty of actually finding something better. They may also be concerned about falling house prices and negative equity.

Filter 2 – Internally and externally referenced

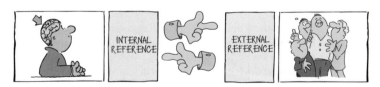

Some people seem to be very confident and positive. They tend to trust their own judgement – they look inside themselves to decide if a particular course of action is correct. Someone who is internally referenced might say

"I just know". By contrast, externally referenced people will be looking to others for confirmation about their thinking, views and decisions. "What do they think?" What do the consumer magazines, papers or blogs say? They tend not to trust their own judgement and tend to rely far more on other people.

Filter 3 – Sameness and difference

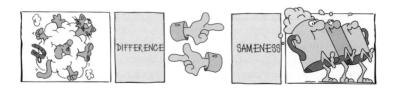

Some people strive for long-term stability in their lives: they stay in the same job, always buy the same make and kind of car, and stay with the same partner for years. They don't like the upheavals that change brings in general and resist it – *sameness* and continuity are important to them.

Difference people may relish change – they'll change jobs on a regular basis. They'll challenge the normal "way we do things round here". They welcome change and the positive influence they can bring by questioning the status quo and taking a fresh look at the way things are done. To sameness people they could be seen as very disruptive!

Filter 4 – Big picture and small picture

Another of my favourite NLP tools. "Chunking" is the ability to look at something at different levels of detail or generalisation. In this cartoon we go from one particular bear, to bears, to animals in general. As with other character traits, people have preferences, habitual ways of making sense of the world. For example, some people, when you're talking to them, tend to get involved in minute detail, *small chunk*; others take a more global view so that they see the overall scheme of things, *big chunk*.

I work as a tutor at a business school. When looking at a business, you can get involved in all levels of detail. It is important to understand the strategy of the business – What do they do? How does this fit into their market-place? Where do they see themselves going? and so on – the big picture. You can chunk right down through all the levels of detail to get a full under-standing of how they operate. For example, in sales (coming down through the levels of detail), why do their customers buy from them? How do they organise the sales department, internal or external sales people? How are salespeople rewarded? What are the details of the commission structure? What cars and other benefits are salespeople given? What model of car entertainment system are salespeople allowed (small picture)?

So how can we use this in everyday communications? For example, when I'm coaching business people, they have a tendency to focus on specific problems, possibly the one that's bothering them most at that moment. It's important that I understand the context of a particular problem, so first I'll get them to "chunk up" so that I fully understand the bigger picture and get a feel for the most appropriate strategy to use. Then we can start to drill down to the specific issue that's troubling them. The interesting thing is that when you do this, it often gives them a different perspective on the issue, and this may open up new possibilities in terms of developing alterna-tive solutions.

Filter 5 – What's the time(scale)?

PAST   PRESENT   FUTURE

111

Although a friend is a good storyteller, his stories can get a bit annoying at times (in other words, he loses rapport with me). For example, on a break with a group of friends, he started recalling incidents from the last holiday. Initially that was fine, but it didn't change. All he wanted to talk about was the past, whereas after ten minutes of this I was thinking, "Never mind the last holiday, let's focus on this trip, on what we're doing right now."

Similarly, but differently, some people are obsessed with the future – they just talk about future plans and dreams – maybe just a holiday, but the dream of winning the lottery can turn into a perpetual daydream. You might hear something like, "It will be all right when I get a new car, or a new job, or a new house, or a new partner ..." They may even live in an improbable or even impossible future. At times this can be fun and it is something most of us do, but it can go too far so that it stops people living for the moment!

I was at my pottery class earlier this week and a man on the next wheel was saying that he loved making pots because it made him forget everything else and just focus on the now. I find painting similar and I imagine that playing a musical instrument could be the same.

Conclusions

So here we have five different ways of understanding how we filter information – ways that colour our views of the world. I've talked about the extremes of each, but it is more useful to think of them as continuums or spectrums.

Although you may notice common patterns of behaviour in yourself and others, it is also the case that the situation you find yourself in will determine which filters are important; and you may find that in another environment, your filter has slipped along the scale from one end to the other. So noticing how other people are at any one time will exercise you in different ways. Remember that they are only snapshots of reality, and not reality itself.

Chapter 13

Choices, Part 1:

Let's look at that another way ...

Introduction

Back to glasses of beer! We've already discussed the fact that you can look at the same glass as being half full or half empty. But suppose you believe it to be half empty, and then were persuaded or just changed your mind to believe that it is half full?

Would you feel different about it?

Would you feel better?

It's the same glass, but you've changed your view or perception of it!

When you look back at your life, you know you've done this many times already. That kid at school that you started off by disliking ... but who became a best friend. The TV programme that you became obsessed with once you got used to the actors' sense of humour.

So can you change your perception on demand? Of course you can. All you need to do is to train yourself to have a number of different perspectives. And some are likely to make you feel better, to offer greater meaning and thus allow you to do things more effectively.

Negative to positive

Driving would be a good example. An incident happens, such as someone cuts you up or tailgates you. At this point, you have a choice. You can choose to swear at the other driver, shake your fist and generally get upset! Does this affect you or the other driver? Who goes into work all hot and bothered and angry – them or you? However, you can also choose to adopt another view. How about if you said to yourself, "I pity him driving like that – he is nowhere near as good a driver as I am!" Would you feel better about yourself and less likely to affect those around you? Probably!

Reg Connolly of Pegasus NLP Training sums it up very well when he says:

A behaviour does not, in itself, have any meaning. You can make it mean or signify anything – especially if you deliver the other point of view with rapport, with creativity and with congruency.

I have found this switching attitudes to be a really powerful tool. "The computer/photocopier/printer/phone/iPod/video/DVD upset me because it

115

didn't know what to do!" is a very negative view. The machine isn't upset, just you. It doesn't help to sort the problem out either. What's an alternative view? How about, "I'm curious as to why that didn't work – I could try something else, ask somebody to help me, or I could even read the manual!"

It works well for relationships too. After a long hard day, particularly when you're tired, it's easy to get upset with other people, especially your children if they've done something you're not happy about. But rather than get upset, how much better to think and say, "Kids, don't you just love them?" This will probably affect you as well as them.

Whatever field of human endeavour you're engaged in, it's very easy to get down, to feel bad about yourself or even to beat yourself up. If things aren't going well, how can you look at life another way? Have a think about it, and come up with some ideas that will help you (or if you've someone else in mind, how you can help them).

When I'm coaching and the client is upset with him or her self, I go back to that good old standby of counting your blessings. They may not have met a particular target, but they did pretty well. They may not have won that order, but the customer was impressed with their proposal and will ask them to compete again for the next order ...

My wife has just tried a new recipe for our lunch, English onion soup. It was good, but not as good as she would have liked. It's the middle of January, so all that vitamin C, in terms of keeping colds away, is excellent! As the Monty Python team said, "Always look on the bright side of life!"

Chapter 14

Choices, Part 2:
I believe ...

Introduction

Do your beliefs help you? Do they support your identity, who you want to be? There are two sorts of belief – those that can stop you and those that can help you. We'll call these *limiting beliefs* and *positive* or *empowering beliefs*.

Limiting beliefs

I can't speak French, drive in London, ride a horse, play the guitar, understand algebra, draw, paint, sing, dance, grow vegetables, speak in public, catch a cricket ball, putt, serve at tennis, swim, pat my head and rub my tummy, understand women, understand men, talk to teenagers, use a computer properly, make small talk, stop eating chocolate, lose weight, cook, stop drinking wine, read a map, call my aunt, find the time to do anything well, throw out my old clothes, tidy the garage, sort out my files, sort out the loft, write a book, learn to use my digital camera, stand the sight of blood, think about my life …

The list is endless! I'm realising as I write this that some of these are "I won't ..." and some of them are "No, I really can't ..." And then I'm thinking, "Is that a real distinction, or one just in my mind?"

By the way, I'm sure none of these apply to you, but maybe you know someone ...

At my junior school when I was about 8, I decided that I wanted to join the school choir. I duly went along to the audition and started singing. The teacher in charge walked around the group of children and eventually stopped by me. She said, "Go and stand by the wall and just listen." I did as I was told and, needless to say, I never joined the choir. What followed was that I believed I was tone deaf and that I couldn't sing. This only lasted for 50 years!

Eventually, three years ago, I got increasingly frustrated by this and asked a hypnotherapist friend if she could help me using hypnosis. She just laughed! In 30 seconds she proved to me that I wasn't tone deaf.

HEALTH WARNING – only try this with someone you know well and who can sing. You just press one of your cheekbones against one of theirs; when they sing a note, miraculously you then copy it spot on!

Now this didn't mean I could sing, but it did mean that I could now learn how to sing.

Do you remember we talked about anchors in Chapter 5? It's almost as if the words "I can't ..." act as an anchor and stop our minds from working. How often when someone (or you or I) says those (un)magic words do we, with a soppy grin on our faces, nod and agree and say, "Yeah, I can't ..."? We just want to switch off and not even think about it. It's a big cop out. And it seems socially acceptable to claim that I can't dance, do maths or whatever, so I just smile and relax! I've joined the club – of losers! And if the limiting belief is challenged, you come back with a response that might be said with the tonality of, "How on earth would you dare to suggest that I could possibly do that!"

IT DOES MY HEAD IN...

Positive beliefs

What's the alternative? I've mentioned that I run a "Drawing for the terrified" class. Just about everyone who comes starts by saying, "I can't draw ..." usually with that soppy smile! What I try to do is get them to change to a way of thinking which says " ... but I could learn to draw."

There's a lot of talk in popular culture that you can have or do anything that you tell yourself you want. While I agree that you need to have a positive outcome (see also the next chapter), you also need something which will get you there or at least starts to get you there.

WHERE ARE YOU NOW?

WHERE ARE YOU GOING?

HOW WILL YOU GET THERE?

This is the concept (or model) that is used at Cranfield Business School. It helps people to get a positive structure to their thinking. For example in a small business:

- Where are you now? – "I run a profitable business, but I'm not happy that I'm getting a sufficient return for my efforts."

- Where are you going? – "Therefore, I want to double my profits over the next five years."

- How will you get there? – "I will start by recruiting a marketing manager to develop our website and e-business."

The approach works not only for developing a strategy for a business, but for everyday things. Good examples would be in sport. Just think of the thousands of people who run marathons now compared to say even 20 years ago.

To be successful at golf, it's better to have a positive thought of how it will feel and sound to hit the ball well, to visualise the flight of the ball and to clearly pinpoint the spot where it will land. Contrast that to thinking, "Don't hit the ball into the lake!" You already know that the mind doesn't recognise negatives, it just hears, "Hit the ball into the water."

A positive belief is as powerful as a limiting belief is, well, limiting!

How then can we make this change (assuming that you want to change)? Well we can start by using some of the ideas from this book :

- What resources do I have available?

- What motivation in terms of away from and towards can I use?

- What can I learn from feedback, both negative (things that didn't work) and positive (things that did work)?

- What can I detect within my feelings about these changes that I want to occur?

- What language am I using (out loud, in my thoughts or with my body) when I consider my options?

- Can I use the concept of chunking to break down a big idea into smaller, more manageable steps? For example, the first steps in "I want to sail round the world" might be I'd better learn to swim and find out if I actually like sailing.

In the next two chapters, we'll look more at defining what it is that you might want and how you can go about achieving it, now that you've got a positive attitude and belief.

Chapter 15

What do I want?

Objectives, goals and all that stuff

In the last chapter we discussed that positive beliefs are so much more powerful than limiting ones. In the same way, when thinking about the outcome (or goal or objective) you want from a particular situation, it's just so much better (= more effective, more empowering) to do this with a positive statement.

For example, you might be thinking "I want to lose weight." You might even make the target specific and timely "I want to lose 7lb in the next eight weeks." You might have heard of or be familiar with the SMART acronym for setting objectives: Specific, Measurable, Achievable, Realistic and Timely. This is used in many organisations and the statement above does indeed meet the guidelines of the acronym.

But, and it's a big but (or a big butt), it is not positively stated! It's an away from target – it's about what I don't want, not what I do want. Can I rephrase it in a positive way? How about "I want to look good in 36 inch waist trousers"? I think this lack of positive statement is one of the reasons why diets (or "weight loss plans") invariably fail.

And not just "I want to lose weight" – most New Year's resolutions, for example, are similarly expressed: "I want to stop smoking" or "I need to drink less" – as opposed to "I want a healthy lifestyle" or "I will have 120 alcohol free days this year." And we all know what happens to New Year's resolutions, don't we?

The only trouble with these positive goals is that you have to think about them! It's challenging to be positive and say what you want rather than what you don't want. "I don't like my job, car, flat or whatever" is much easier than working out want you want instead. If you claim, "I just want it to be different" then it probably will be different in an unexpected and possibly undesirable way! And what about the really big questions like "What do I want to do with my career, relationships or even, life!" Here are a couple of ideas that might help.

A postcard from me to me …

Try writing a postcard to yourself from the future. I know that this is unusual, if not downright weird, but you can do this! Describe your life in five years' time. Assume that this is a time when you've achieved your goals and notice what's different:

■   What do you see?

■   What sounds do you hear?

■   What can you smell and taste?

■   What does it feel like to be there?

■   If you could draw a picture of what it's like, what would it look like? What would happen if you had a go at drawing it now?

My perfect day

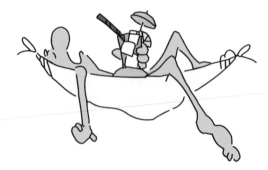

Take today's date and add ten years to it – for example, it's 1st February 2008, so make it 1st February 2018 (over five years since the London Olympic games!). Describe your perfect day:

■ Where are you?

■ Who are you with?

■ What are you doing?

■ What are you able to do now that you couldn't do before?

■ Which of your beliefs and values have changed?

■ Who are you now?

The more detail and the more you can use all your senses to imagine this, the more powerful it might be. Take a good, long time to think about this – go on, indulge yourself!

If you've tried one or both of these techniques, they should have given you a sense of what you want long term (or you might already have a good idea of your future plans).

Use this as your starting point (well, actually it's an end point, but you know what I mean) and work back towards today. If you will have achieved x in five years' time, where will you have got to in four, three, two, one years' time? If you've now developed an intermediate stage for the long-term goal that's set in one year, where might you be in six months, or three months or even next month? If that's where you've got to be in a month's time, what do you need to this week? To make that happen this week, what do you need to start doing right now?

Do you get the idea? It's like the concept of chunking from Chapter 12, but applied to timescales ...

Chapter 16

How to do it and final thoughts ...

Introduction

You now know about some of the vital tools that come in the NLP toolbox. But just having the tools won't get you very far; you actually have to use them. And the best place to start is with yourself. So the final task is to consider how you can turn the thinking processes covered in this book into the changes that you want to make.

Think/plan/do

Everything starts with a thought. Everything we do, every object, just about everything that is around you was once an idea in someone's mind. Mankind makes things happen in the world. For the idea to be turned into action, we need to plan how to make that happen. The more thorough the planning, the more likely we are to achieve the final outcome (unless you're just trying to be spontaneous). Lastly comes the "doing" part I think this is the most challenging part.

This is where that fabulous animal, procrastination, rears its ugly head! But go back to Chapter 2 and those ten interesting ideas: if "there's no failure, only feedback" then what's stopping you? What's the worst that could happen? So have a go: you've thought about it, planned it – now, just do it! Read on for more ideas on how to make this happen ...

The NLP action process (the doing bit!)

This is a suggested NLP model (or process or idea) to help you make things happen and take that all important action. As an example, I've tried to draw the idea of going from an undesired state (unhappy) to a desired state (happy). What do I need to do to make this happen? What resources can I draw upon? A resource could be from the internet, a book, a friend, someone from my past who had a particular relevant skill, an imaginary character, someone from TV or film, a fictional character, someone from history – the list is endless! See also Idea 3 in Chapter 2. How flexible am I prepared to be? What limiting beliefs could I put aside? What do my senses tell me, for example, if I try my idea out on someone whose opinion I respect (how do I think that they're reacting)?

How have I applied this process ? Well, one example would be about a request from a client to provide "light relief, oh and team spirit" at a half-day in-house conference that they were planning to hold just before Christmas. I quickly established the basic facts of where the event would be held, how many people they thought would be attending and how much time I was to be allocated. I had some team activities that I thought would be suitable and quickly researched some more on the web. Two team building books were ordered from Amazon and duly arrived (one was excellent, one was not so useful). I rushed down to the local Toys-R-Us shop to buy the necessary resources for some of the games (I mean team building activities). I prepared my contribution and eventually the day arrived.

There were about 16 people there, as opposed to the 30 I had planned for. Being flexible, I rescheduled my games. What I hadn't realised was that this particular Friday afternoon was part Christmas party and alcohol was freely available. I quickly got the feedback from the first two exercises, about what the audience liked and wanted more of! More flexibility in adjusting the programme again (it helps to be really well prepared to do this quickly and easily). The end result was a group who really enjoyed their afternoon and a satisfied client!

Go on, have a go at applying the NLP action process.

And lastly, a Gandhi story ...

One time, a woman came to Gandhi and asked him to tell her over-weight son to stop eating sugar.

"Madam," he replied, "come back in three weeks' time."

Surprised at this request, she nevertheless returned with her son three weeks later.

Gandhi looked at the boy and said, "Stop eating sugar."

When the boy had left the room, the mother turned to Ghandi and asked why he hadn't said this three weeks ago.

Gandhi replied, "Madam, three weeks ago I myself was eating sugar."

The point of the story is that it is easy to talk (or even write a book about it), but actually doing something, actually deciding to change your life and/or make a difference for others isn't easy, but I hope *The Really Good Fun Cartoon Book of NLP* has been enjoyable and has made the journey a little easier.

Appendices

Notes

Throughout the book I've avoided NLP jargon. In these notes you will find a guide to the NLP language that I've assiduously avoided in the main part of the book.

Introduction

1. The Cartoons. The actual cartoon characters were drawn by my old friend, the cartoonist, Robert Duncan (www.duncancartoons.com).

Chapter 1

4. NLP was developed by two academics, Richard Bandler and Dr John Grinder at the University of Santa Cruz in California in the 1970s. They modelled the communication skills of Milton Erickson (a clinical hypnotherapist), Virginia Satir (a family therapist) and Fritz Perls (the founder of Gestalt therapy). They also studied linguists and philosophers, as well as becoming students of life – noticing what people actually did when they communicated.

7. Start with the end in mind. This is a quote by Steven Covey in *The Seven Habits of Highly Effective People*, Simon & Schuster Ltd; rev. ed (1999).

9. Ways which might be considered unethical. One way to think about this is whether you are doing things solely for your own benefit, or whether you are considering the benefit to the other person.

Chapter 2

11. Ten interesting ideas. These are a subset of the so-called NLP Presuppositions.

13. "Fail, fail again, fail better". Samuel Beckett, Irish writer, 1906–1989.

16. Bryn Terfel. Biography: www.bbc.co.uk/wales/music/sites/brynterfel/pages/biography.html

17. Betty Edwards. Betty Edwards (2002) *New Drawing on the Right Side of the Brain Workbook*, Souvenir Press.

Chapter 3

26. The personality (onion) or map is my take on the NLP logical levels or neurological levels (developed by Robert Dilts) which are based loosely on the work of the philosopher Bertrand Russell and the anthropologist Gregory Bateson.

Chapter 4

38. We'd add more description. The distinctions made for each of the senses – the qualities of the experience – are referred to in NLP as "sub-modalities".

41. Heston Blumenthal. Heston Blumenthal: *In Search Of Perfection*, broadcast on Wednesday, 19 December 2007, BBC Two, 8pm.

Chapter 5

44. Anchors. An anchor is a trigger or stimulus that produces a certain response, every time it occurs.

42. I was singing "Oklahoma". The significance of Oklahoma, in terms of this book/NLP is that when I remember (an anchor recalled) the event, I experience the pleasure again and a sense of pride in what I, a previous non-singer, achieved that day! See also the note to Chapter 9. How I got involved in the choir is in Chapter 14.

48. *Rick Stein's Mediterranean Escapes*. Broadcast on BBC Two in November/December 2007.

    Book: *Rick Stein's Mediterranean Escapes*, BBC Books (2007)
    ISBN-10: 0563493666
    ISBN-13: 978-0563493662

47. The minimise button. This is my version of the NLP technique called the swish pattern.

Chapter 6

52. The fly-on-the-wall perspective is sometimes called the "meta position". The process of the two chairs was developed by Fritz Perls, one of the excellent communicators upon whose work NLP was developed. This way of systematically going round these different points of view is sometimes referred to as the meta-mirror.

53. We tend to see things very much from our point of view. This is probably more true of men; women tend to be more considerate of how

others are feeling, especially when they are looking after babies and children.

Chapter 7

58. I think that woman are better at this. Again, they are better able to put themselves in the other person's shoes, and in general, women tend to seek more collaborative solutions, whereas men vie for dominance.

60. Reg Connolly at Pegasus NLP Training. I trained with Reg Connolly for 4 years, and appreciated his style of teaching. For further details: see Appendix, Pg 147.

62. Who looks at the ground the whole time. In some cultures it is considered bad form to make eye contact, so be sensitive to other people's traditions and needs .

Chapter 9

This chapter is all about the NLP meta-model of language.

88 "Out of the blue". Was this really an amazing coincidence, or was it more because we had set a clear outcome (see Chapter 15) and maintained the positive attitude that it would be fulfilled – in a surprising, unexpected way?

Chapter 10

92. It's how you say it. This chapter is all about the Milton Model (named after Milton Erickson) and explores how you can use language to get other people to do things with minimal resistance.

93. Notice the difference. Notice the physiology – where you head goes when you say these. "Tell me" is more forward; "I'm curious" is more head back, possibly at an angle ...

94. "Don't". Think about stories you heard as a child, how many of them had a forbidden activity: don't look back, don't open the box, don't go through that door ... knowing full well that that is exactly what's going to happen.

98. People love stories and metaphors. When you tell people stories they relax and become more open to suggestion, more open to learning in an unconscious way.

98. A repertoire of useful stories and metaphors. Plenty on the internet, and Nick Owen's books are a good place to start.

Chapter 11 Language without words

102. Catherine Tate is broadcast on BBC television. Catherine Tate is an English actress and comedienne whose BBC Two solo series *The Catherine Tate show* began in 2004. See: http://www.catherinetate.co.uk/

104. The eyes also tell us a lot. Part of this discussion concerns what in NLP are called eye-accessing cues – a subject not without controversy. Sometimes you see them, sometimes you don't.

Chapter 12

108. How we filter information. This is all about the NLP concept of metaprograms – distinctions we can make about how people sort information about the world, and how the typical behaviours they engage in when they do things in the world. NLP uses the metaphor of "filter" to describe these characteristics, based on the notion that we select some things and exclude others.

108 Myers-Briggs Type Indicator (MBTI)
www.myersbriggs.org/my-mbti-personality-type/mbti-basics/

108 Belbin
www.belbin.com

108 Thomas International (DISC)
www.thomas.co.uk

Chapter 13

116. Look at life another way. This is all about "frames" and "reframing".

117. Monty Python. This song was used in the Monty Python movie *Life of Brian* (1979) directed by Terry Jones.

Chapter 14

122. How will you get there? This is about strategies ...

Chapter 15

126. SMART. In NLP goal-setting is called well-formed outcomes.

Chapter 16

133. The NLP action process. This material draws on the NLP concept of resources – all the things in your experience – your capabilities, know-how – that can be utilised for achieving a new goal, just so long as you can generalise from the specific event in the past to the new situation.

135. A Gandhi story. This is based on a traditional Sufi story about the Mulla Nasrudin, which has been around for several hundred years. For some reason it is now usually attributed to Gandhi, but that could be because it ties in neatly with a quote attributed to him which says, "You must be the change you wish to see in the world."

Bibliography

These are some of the books that I've found interesting and helpful:

Gillian Burn (2005) *The NLP Pocketbook*, Management Pocketbooks
ISBN-10: 1903776317
ISBN-13: 978-1903776315

Betty Edwards (2001) *The New Drawing on the Right Side of the Brain*, Harper Collins Publishers Ltd; 3rd rev. edn
ISBN-10: 0007116454
ISBN-13: 978-0007116454

Claire Gordon (2005) *The Personality Profiler*, Carroll & Brown Publishers Limited
ISBN-10: 1904760147
ISBN-13: 978-1904760146

Sue Knight (2002) *NLP at Work: The Difference that Makes a Difference in Business*, Nicholas Brealey Publishing Ltd; 2nd rev, edn edition
ISBN-10: 1857883020
ISBN-13: 978-1857883022

Max Landsberg (2003) *Tao of Coaching: Boost Your Effectiveness at Work* by Inspiring and Developing Those Around You, Profile Business; new edn
ISBN-10: 186197650X
ISBN-13: 978-1861976505

Paul McKenna (2006) *Instant Confidence*, Bantam Press
ISBN-10: 0593055357
ISBN-13: 978-0593055359

Nick Owen (2001) *The Magic of Metaphor: 77 Stories for Teachers, Trainers and Thinkers*, Crown House Publishing
ISBN-10 1899836705
ISBN-13 978-1899836703

Nick Owen (2004) *More Magic of Metaphor: Stories for Leaders, Influencers and Motivators*, Crown House Publishing
ISBN-10 1904424414
ISBN-13 978-1904424413

Romilla Ready & Kate Burton (2004) *Neuro-linguistic Programming for Dummies*, John Wiley & Sons
ISBN-10: 0764570285
ISBN-13: 978-0764570285

Julie Starr (2007) *The Coaching Manual: The Definitive Guide to the Process, Principles and Skills of Personal Coaching*, Prentice Hall; 2nd edn
ISBN-10: 0273713523
ISBN-13: 978-0273713524

NLP training

There are many NLP training companies. I've had most personal experience with two trainers that I can recommend:

In the south of England:

Reg Connolly at Pegasus NLP Training
www.nlp-now.co.uk

In the north of England:

Derek Jackson at the Northern School of NLP
www.nlpand.co.uk

About the cartoons

The cartoon characters were drawn by my old friend, the cartoonist Robert Duncan (www.duncancartoons.com).

They're available on CD-ROM from Bitfolio Limited, the clipart software company. Details as follows:

Windows, Macintosh and Acorn versions

Telephone
(+44 20 7439 0400)

Fax
(+44 20 7439 0300)

E-mail
sales@bitfolio.com

Post
Bitfolio Ltd, 77 Oxford Street, London, W1R 1RB, United Kingdom

Contact details

Philip Miller
Telephone: 0118 940 6867
E-mail: Philipmillernlp@aol.com

Praise for

The Really
Good Fun Cartoon
Book of NLP

"This book lives up to its name. It is clear and easy to read, and explains the key NLP principles in a fun way. The cartoons and stories enhance the messages giving you a greater understanding, and even a smile along the way."

GILLIAN BURN, DIRECTOR, HEALTH CIRCLES LTD, AUTHOR OF THE NLP POCKETBOOK AND THE ENERGY AND WELL-BEING POCKETBOOK

" A terrific little book for anyone curious to find out what the acronym 'NLP' is all about. The text is easy to read and the anecdotes and cartoons are a great way to re-enforce the learning. The NLP toolbox is broken into small, manageable steps that can be incorporated into everyday life to make living easier."

ROMILLA READY CO-AUTHOR OF NEURO-LINGUISTIC PROGRAMMING FOR DUMMIES®

"I love this book. It is simple, fun, creative and above all an open door to everything that NLP seeks to represent in a way that just encourages you to want to learn more. And it is presented in a way that suits the learning style of a large part of the population - me included!"

SUE KNIGHT AUTHOR OF NLP AT WORK, INTERNATIONAL NLP TRAINER AND COACH - WWW.SUEKNIGHT.COM

"Phil has written and illustrated a little gem in *The Really Good Fun Cartoon Book of NLP*. In less than 160 pages he has covered a huge amount of ground and, unlike a lot of NLP books, he has done this in jargon-free plain English and with lots of anecdotes and stories to being the ideas to life. It's also easy on the eye. The prolific cartoons ensure that you're not faced with page after page of dull blocks of text.

A "cartoon book" it may be, and it's certainly well illustrated with cartoons, but it's no 'light-weight' – it's well written and the material is accessible to just about anyone.

Being a bit lazy, and to help me review it, I asked some of the participants on one of our recent NLP Practitioner Certification Courses to read
the book and let me have their comments. Interestingly enough, all of the
comments were positive. They said they would like to be able to give it to
family and friends to give them a taster of what's included in a Practitioner
Course – but they would also like to keep a copy for themselves to quickly
refresh their knowledge from time to time!"

REG CONNOLLY, TRAINING DIRECTOR, PEGASUS NLP